The Complete Sausage Cookbook

Sausage Recipes Made Simple

By

Angel Burns

© 2019 Angel Burns, All Rights Reserved.

License Notices

This book or parts thereof might not be reproduced in any format for personal or commercial use without the written permission of the author. Possession and distribution of this book by any means without said permission is prohibited by law.

All content is for entertainment purposes and the author accepts no responsibility for any damages, commercially or personally, caused by following the content.

Get Your Daily Deals Here!

Free books on me! Subscribe now to receive free and discounted books directly to your email. This means you will always have choices of your next book from the comfort of your own home and a reminder email will pop up a few days beforehand, so you never miss out! Every day, free books will make their way into your inbox and all you need to do is choose what you want.

What could be better than that?

Fill out the box below to get started on this amazing offer and start receiving your daily deals right away!

https://angel-burns.gr8.com

Table of Contents

Easy and Delicious Sausage Recipes 6

Recipe 1: Gravy and Sausage Casserole 7

Recipe 2: Wild Rice and Sausage Mushroom Soup 10

Recipe 3: Spicy Brown Butter Sausage Alfredo 13

Recipe 4: Italian Sausage Orzo 16

Recipe 5: Feta Mushroom Sausage Burgers 19

Recipe 6: Italian Sausage Zucchini Soup 22

Recipe 7: Italian Sausage Sandwiches 25

Recipe 8: Roasted Potatoes, Sausage and Asparagus ... 28

Recipe 9: Turkey Sausage Bean Soup 31

Recipe 10: Greek Breakfast Sausage Casserole 34

Recipe 11: Quinoa and Sausage Peppers 37

Recipe 12: Sausage and Pepper Fettuccine 40

Recipe 13: Sausage and Greens Soup 43

Recipe 14: Caribbean Sausage Chicken Stew 46

Recipe 15: Turkey and Sausage Cabbage Rolls 49

Recipe 16: Sausage and Mushroom Rigatoni 52

Recipe 17: Sausage Jambalaya 55

Recipe 18: Sausage and Egg Grits 58

Recipe 19: Sausage and Egg Burritos 61

Recipe 20: Smoked Sausage and Potato Soup 64

Recipe 21: Italian Sausage and Potato Chowder 67

Recipe 22: Apple and Sausage Salad with Vinaigrette . 70

Recipe 23: Andouille Sausage Soup 73

Recipe 24: One Pot Cajun Chicken and Sausage Alfredo 76

Recipe 25: One Pan Smoked Sausage and Pasta 79

About the Author 82

Author's Afterthoughts 84

Easy and Delicious Sausage Recipes

HHHHHHHHHHHHHHHHHHHHHHHHHHHHHHH

Recipe 1: Gravy and Sausage Casserole

This is a sausage dish that is sure to be a sure crowd-pleaser. It is a casserole dish you can make for breakfast to kick off your morning in a filling way.

Yield: 6 servings

Preparation Time: 35 minutes

Ingredient List:

- 1 can of flaky biscuits
- 1 pound of ground Italian sausage
- 3 Tablespoons of all-purpose flour
- 2 ½ cups of whole milk
- Dash of salt and black pepper

HHHHHHHHHHHHHHHHHHHHHHHHHHHHHH

Instructions:

1. Heat the oven to 400 degrees. Grease a baking dish.

2. Slice the flaky biscuits into quarters and place into the bottom of the baking dish.

3. Place into the oven to bake for 8 to 10 minutes or until browned.

4. In a skillet set over medium to high heat, add in the ground Italian sausage. Cook for 5 to 8 minutes or until browned. Add in the all-purpose flour. Whisk until mixed. Continue to cook for an additional 3 to 4 minutes.

5. Add in the whole milk. Season with a dash of salt and black pepper. Allow to come to a low boil. Cook for 3 minutes or until thick in consistency.

6. Pour over the top of the biscuits.

7. Place into the oven to bake for 10 minutes. Cover with a sheet of aluminum foil and continue to bake for an additional 10 minutes or until the biscuits are browned.

8. Remove and serve immediately.

Recipe 2: Wild Rice and Sausage Mushroom Soup

This is a filling soup that makes for a perfect weeknight or weekend dinner. Serve in a bread bowl for even tastier results.

Yield: 8 servings

Preparation Time: 1 hour and 10 minutes

Recipe 3: Spicy Brown Butter Sausage Alfredo

Make this delicious dish whenever you want to spoil your family with something extra special. Serve with a salad for the tastiest results.

Yield: 4 servings

Preparation Time: 35 minutes

Ingredient List:

- 8 ounces of pappardelle pasta
- 3 links of spicy Italian sausage, casings removed and thinly sliced
- 1 clove of garlic, grated
- ¼ cup of butter
- 1 cup of heavy whipping cream
- 1 cup of parmigiano Reggiano cheese, grated
- Dash of salt and black pepper
- Parsley, chopped and for garnish

HHHHHHHHHHHHHHHHHHHHHHHHHHHHHHH

Instructions:

1. Prepare the pappardelle pasta according to the directions on the package. Once cooked, drain the pasta and set aside.

2. In a skillet, add in the sliced Italian sausage. Cook for 8 to 10 minutes or until browned. Transfer onto a plate and set aside. Drain the excess grease.

3. Add in the butter. Cook for 1 to 2 minutes or until browned. Add in the grated garlic. Cook for an additional 30 seconds.

4. Add in the heavy whipping cream and grated parmigiano Reggiano cheese. Stir well to mix. Cook for 1 to 2 minutes.

5. Add in the cooked Italian sausage. Season with a dash of salt and black pepper.

6. Add in the cooked pasta and toss to coat.

7. Remove from heat. Serve with a garnish of chopped parsley.

Recipe 4: Italian Sausage Orzo

This is a light and hearty sausage dish you can make any night of the week. It is so delicious, I guarantee you will want to make it as often as possible.

Yield: 6 servings

Preparation Time: 40 minutes

Ingredient List:

- 8 cups of water
- 3 teaspoons of low sodium chicken bouillon granules
- 1 ½ cups of whole wheat orzo pasta
- 1, 19.5 ounce pack of Italian turkey sausage links, casings removed
- ½ cup of sweet onion, chopped
- 2 cloves of garlic, minced
- 3 plum tomatoes, chopped
- ½ cup of roasted sweet red peppers, chopped
- Dash of salt and black pepper
- 1/8 teaspoons of crushed red pepper flakes
- 1/3 cup of basil, chopped
- ¼ cup of grated Parmesan cheese

HHHHHHHHHHHHHHHHHHHHHHHHHHHHHHH

Instructions:

1. In a saucepan set over medium to high heat, add in the water and chicken bouillon granules. Allow to come to a boil. Add in the whole wheat orzo pasta. Allow to come back to a boil. Cook for 8 to 10 minutes or until soft. Drain the pasta and set aside. Reserve ¾ cup of the pasta liquid.

2. In a skillet set over medium heat, grease with cooking spray. Add in the sausage, chopped onion and minced garlic. Cook for 6 to 8 minutes or until browned.

3. Add in the chopped plum tomatoes, crushed red pepper flakes, cooked orzo pasta and roasted sweet red pepper. Season with a dash of salt and black pepper. Stir well to mix. Continue to cook for 5 to 10 minutes or until the pepper is soft.

4. Remove from heat.

5. Add in the chopped basil and grated Parmesan cheese. Stir well to incorporate.

6. Serve immediately.

Recipe 5: Feta Mushroom Sausage Burgers

There is nothing more filling then this delicious burger dish. Make during your next family barbecue whenever you want to spoil the entire family.

Yield: 6 servings

Preparation Time: 25 minutes

Ingredient List:

- 1 pound of lean ground beef
- 3 Italian sausage links, casings removed
- 2 teaspoons of Worcestershire sauce
- ½ teaspoons of powdered garlic
- 2 Tablespoons of balsamic vinegar
- 1 tablespoon of extra virgin olive oil
- 6 portobello mushrooms, stems removed
- 1 onion, thinly sliced
- 6 Tablespoons of feta cheese, crumbled
- 6 whole wheat hamburger buns, split open
- 10 basil leaves, thinly sliced

HHHHHHHHHHHHHHHHHHHHHHHHHHHHHHH

Instructions:

1. In a bowl, add in the lean ground beef, Italian sausage, Worcestershire sauce and powdered garlic. Stir well until mixed.

2. Shape this mix into 6 burger patties that are ½ an inch in thickness.

3. In a separate bowl, add in the balsamic vinegar and olive oil. Stir well to mix. Brush over the top of the burger patties.

4. Place onto a preheated outdoor grill to cook over medium heat for 5 minutes on both sides or until cooked to your desired doneness.

5. Place the mushrooms and onion onto the grill. Cook for 5 to 8 minutes or until the onions are caramelized.

6. Transfer the burgers, mushrooms and onions onto the hamburger buns.

7. Top off with the crumbled feta cheese and sliced basil leaves.

8. Serve immediately.

Recipe 6: Italian Sausage Zucchini Soup

One bite of this soup dish and you will begin to feel better in no time at all. Once you get a taste of it, it will remind you of your childhood days.

Yield: 10 servings

Preparation Time: 1 hour and 5 minutes

Ingredient List:

- 1, 19.5 ounce pack of sweet Italian turkey sausage links, casings removed
- 4 ribs of celery, chopped
- 1 onion, chopped
- 2 teaspoons of Italian seasoning
- 1 teaspoon of dried oregano
- ½ teaspoons of salt
- ½ teaspoons of powdered garlic
- ½ teaspoons of dried basil
- 2 zucchinis, cut into small cubes
- 2 green bell peppers, thinly sliced
- 4, 14.5-ounce cans of whole tomatoes, crushed
- 1, 14.5 ounce can of low sodium chicken broth
- 1 teaspoon of white sugar

HHHHHHHHHHHHHHHHHHHHHHHHHHHHHHH

Instructions:

1. In a stockpot set over medium to high heat, add in the Italian sausage. Crumble slightly. Cook for 6 to 8 minutes or until the sausage is browned. Remove and transfer onto a plate. Set aside. Drain the excess grease.

2. In the pot, add in the chopped celery, chopped onion, Italian seasoning, dried oregano, dash of salt, powdered garlic and dried basil. Stir gently to mix. Cook for 5 minutes or until soft.

3. Add in the cooked sausage, chopped zucchini cubes, sliced green bell peppers, crushed tomatoes, low sodium chicken broth and white sugar. Stir well to mix.

4. Cover and lower the heat to low. Cook for 30 minutes or until the zucchini and bell peppers are soft.

5. Remove from heat and serve immediately.

Recipe 7: Italian Sausage Sandwiches

Once you get a taste of these sandwiches, I guarantee you will never want to make regular boring sandwiches ever again.

Yield: 4 servings

Preparation Time: 30 minutes

Ingredients for the butter:

- ½ cup of butter, soft
- ¼ cup of basil, chopped
- ¼ cup of parsley, chopped
- 1 teaspoon of garlic paste

Ingredients for the sausage

- 1 pound of ground Italian sausage
- 1, 14 ounce can of tomato sauce
- ¼ cup of red wine
- Dash of salt
- 1 tablespoon of basil, chopped

Ingredients for the sandwiches:

- 4 hot dog buns
- 4 slices of mozzarella cheese
- 8 slices of provolone cheese
- Red onion, chopped and for garnish
- Basil, chopped and for garnish

HHHHHHHHHHHHHHHHHHHHHHHHHHHHHH

Instructions:

1. Prepare the butter. In a bowl, add in all of the ingredients for the butter. Stir well to mix. Cover and set into the fridge until ready for use.

2. Prepare the sausage mix. In a skillet set over medium heat, add in the ground Italian sausage. Cook for 8 to 10 minutes or until browned. Add in the can of tomato sauce and red wine. Stir well to mix. Allow to simmer for 15 minutes. Remove from heat.

3. Add in the chopped basil. Season with a dash of salt.

4. Spread the butter along the insides of the hot dog buns. Toast in the own for 1 minute.

5. Add a slice of mozzarella cheese onto each hot dog bun. Add a layer of the sausage mix along with 2 slices of provolone cheese.

6. Place back into the oven to broil for 1 minute or until the cheese bubbles.

7. Remove. Top off with the chopped red onion and chopped basil.

8. Serve.

Recipe 8: Roasted Potatoes, Sausage and Asparagus

This is an easy family friendly meal whenever you need to get dinner on the table. It is so delicious, I guarantee it will disappear in a matter of minutes.

Yield: 4 servings

Preparation Time: 40 minutes

Ingredient List:

- 1 pound of baby red potatoes, cut into halves
- 8 ounces of petite baby carrots
- 1 teaspoon of dried basil
- 1 teaspoon of dried thyme
- 1 teaspoon of dried oregano
- 1 teaspoon of smoked paprika
- ½ teaspoons of powdered onion
- Dash of salt and black pepper
- ¼ cup of extra virgin olive oil, separated
- 2 cups of asparagus, ends trimmed
- ½ of a yellow onion, chopped
- 1, 13-ounce pack of smoked sausage, skinless and sliced into coins
- 1 tablespoon of garlic, minced
- 1/3 cup of grated Parmesan cheese
- Parsley, chopped and for garnish

HHHHHHHHHHHHHHHHHHHHHHHHHHHHHH

Instructions:

1. Preheat the oven to 400 degrees. Place a sheet of parchment paper onto a baking sheet.

2. In a bowl, add in the dried basil, dried thyme, dried oregano, smoked paprika, powdered onion, dash of salt and black pepper. Stir well to mix.

3. Add the baby red potato halves and baby carrots onto the baking sheet. Drizzle 2 tablespoons of the olive oil over the potatoes and carrots. Sprinkle half of the seasoning over the top. Toss well to mix.

4. Place into the oven to bake for 20 minutes

5. Push the carrots and potatoes to one side of the baking sheet. On the clear side, add the chopped asparagus, onion slices, smoked sausage coins and minced garlic. Drizzle 2 tablespoons of olive oil over the top along with the remaining seasoning mix. Toss to mix.

6. Place into the oven to bake for an additional 10 to 15 minutes or until soft.

7. Remove. Serve with a topping of grated parmesan cheese and chopped parsley.

Recipe 9: Turkey Sausage Bean Soup

Make this delicious soup recipe whenever you are feeling under the weather. Be sure to serve this soup with a side salad for the healthiest results.

Yield: 8 servings

Preparation Time: 40 minutes

Ingredient List:

- 4 Italian turkey sausage links, casings removed
- 1 onion, chopped
- 1 cup of fennel bulb, chopped
- 1 cup of celery roots, peeled and chopped
- 1, 14.5 ounce can of no salt tomatoes, chopped
- 3 cups of water
- 4 bay leaves
- 1 tablespoon of low sodium beef base
- 2 teaspoons of Italian seasoning
- ½ teaspoons of black pepper
- 2, 15-ounce cans of cannellini beans, drained
- Shaved parmesan cheese, for topping

HHHHHHHHHHHHHHHHHHHHHHHHHHHHHHH

Instructions:

1. In a Dutch oven set over medium heat, add in the turkey sausage links, chopped onion, chopped fennel bulb and chopped celery. Stir well to mix. Cook for 5 minutes or until the sausage is browned.

2. Add in the chopped tomatoes, water, bay leaves, low sodium beef base, dash of black pepper and Italian seasoning. Stir well to mix.

3. Allow to come to a boil. Lower the heat to low and cover. Cook for 20 minutes or until the veggies are soft.

4. Add in the cans of cannellini beans. Stir well to mix. Cook for an additional 2 to 3 minutes or until piping hot.

5. Remove from heat.

6. Serve immediately with a topping of shaved parmesan cheese.

Recipe 10: Greek Breakfast Sausage Casserole

This is the perfect sausage recipe for you to make whenever you need to satisfy a large group of people during the weekend.

Yield: 6 servings

Preparation Time: 1 hour and 25 minutes

Ingredient List:

- ½ pound of Italian sausage links, casings removed
- ½ cup of green bell pepper, chopped
- 1 shallot, chopped
- 1 cup of artichoke hearts, chopped
- 1 cup of broccoli, chopped
- 1/3 cup of sun-dried tomatoes, chopped
- 6 eggs
- 6 egg whites
- 3 Tablespoons of fat free milk
- ½ teaspoons of Italian seasoning
- ¼ teaspoons of powdered garlic
- ¼ teaspoons of black pepper
- 1/3 cup of feta cheese, crumbled

HHHHHHHHHHHHHHHHHHHHHHHHHHHHHH

Instructions:

1. Preheat the oven to 350 degrees.

2. In a skillet set over medium to high heat, add in the Italian sausage, chopped green bell pepper and chopped shallot. Stir well to mix. Cook for 8 to 10 minutes or until the sausage is cooked through. Drain the excess grease. Transfer into a greased baking dish.

3. Top off the artichoke hearts, chopped broccoli and chopped tomatoes.

4. In a bowl, add in the eggs, egg whites, fat free milk, Italian seasoning, powdered garlic and dash of black pepper. Whisk well until mixed.

5. Sprinkle the crumbled feta cheese over the top.

6. Place into the oven to bake for 45 to 50 minutes or until baked through.

7. Remove and cool for 10 minutes before serving.

Recipe 11: Quinoa and Sausage Peppers

If you love the taste of traditional stuffed peppers, then this is a dish I know you are not going to be able to resist.

Yield: 4 servings

Preparation Time: 30 minutes

Ingredient List:

- 1 ½ cups of vegetable stock
- ¾ cup of quinoa
- 1 pound of Italian turkey sausage links, casings removed
- 1 sweet red pepper, chopped
- 1 green bell pepper, seeds removed and chopped
- ¾ cup of sweet onions, chopped
- 1 clove of garlic, minced
- ¼ teaspoons of garam masala
- Dash of salt and black pepper

HHHHHHHHHHHHHHHHHHHHHHHHHHHHHHHH

Instructions:

1. In a saucepan set over medium to high heat, add in the vegetable stock. Allow to come to a boil. Add in the quinoa. Lower the heat to low. Cover and cook for 10 to 15 minutes or until cooked through. Remove from heat and set aside.

2. In a skillet set over medium to high heat, add in the Italian sausage, chopped sweet red pepper, chopped green bell pepper and chopped sweet onions. Stir gently to mix. Cook for 8 to 10 minutes or until the sausage is browned.

3. Add in the minced garlic and garam masala. Season with a dash of salt and black pepper. Cook for an additional minute.

4. Add in the cooked quinoa and stir well to mix.

5. Remove from heat and serve immediately.

Recipe 12: Sausage and Pepper Fettuccine

This is a quick and easy pasta and sausage dish you can make whenever you are craving homemade Italian food.

Yield: 6 servings

Preparation Time: 35 minutes

Ingredient List:

- 8 to 12 ounces of fettuccine pasta
- 2 cups of sweet bell pepper, seeds removed and chopped
- ¾ cup of onion, peeled and chopped
- 2 cups of smoked sausage, thinly sliced
- 1/3 cup of parsley, chopped
- ¾ cup of heavy whipping cream
- 1 cup of pasta water
- 1 cup of chicken broth
- 1 tablespoon of garlic, chopped
- ½ cup of cherry tomatoes, cut in half
- Extra virgin olive oil, as needed

HHHHHHHHHHHHHHHHHHHHHHHHHHHHHHH

Instructions:

1. Prepare the fettuccine according to the directions on the package. Drain the fettuccine and set aside. Reserve 1 cup of the pasta water.

2. In a skillet set over medium to high heat, add in 2 tablespoons of olive oil. Add in the chopped sweet bell pepper and onion. Cook for 5 to 8 minutes or until soft.

3. Add in the sausage. Continue to cook for 6 to 8 minutes or until browned.

4. Add in the chopped garlic. Continue to cook for an additional minute.

5. Add in the pasta water, heavy whipping cream, chicken broth. Stir well to mix. Cook for 5 minutes.

6. Add in the cooked fettuccine, chopped parsley and chopped tomatoes. Continue to cook for 3 to 5 minutes or until thick in consistency.

7. Remove from heat and serve immediately.

Recipe 13: Sausage and Greens Soup

This is a delicious and filling soup recipe you can make whenever you have plenty of vegetables on hand and are craving something incredibly delicious.

Yield: 6 servings

Preparation Time: 40 minutes

Ingredient List:

- 1 tablespoon of extra virgin olive oil
- 2 Italian turkey sausage links, casings removed
- 1 onion, chopped
- 1 rib of celery, chopped
- 1 carrot, chopped
- 1 clove of garlic, minced
- 6 ounces of Swiss chard, chopped
- 1, 14.5 ounce can of tomatoes, chopped and drained
- 1 bay leaf
- 1 teaspoon of rubbed sage
- 1 teaspoon of Italian seasoning
- ½ teaspoons of black pepper
- 1, 32-ounce carton of low sodium chicken broth
- 1, 15 ounce can of cannellini beans, drained
- 1 tablespoon of lemon juice

HHHHHHHHHHHHHHHHHHHHHHHHHHHHHHHH

Ingredient List:

- ½ cup of wild rice
- 1 ½ cups of water
- 8 ounces of smoked turkey sausage, thinly sliced
- 1/3 cup of all-purpose flour
- 1, 32 ounce carton of low sodium chicken broth, evenly divided
- 2 Tablespoons of butter
- 1 onion, chopped
- ½ pound of mushrooms, thinly sliced
- 1 cup of whole milk
- ¼ teaspoons of black pepper

HHHHHHHHHHHHHHHHHHHHHHHHHHHHHHH

Instructions:

1. In a saucepan set over medium to high heat, add in the wild rice and water. Allow to come to a boil. Lower the heat to low. Cook for 40 to 45 minutes or until the rice is soft.

2. In a separate saucepan set over medium to high heat, add in the sliced smoked sausage. Cook for 5 minutes or until browned. Transfer into a bowl and set aside.

3. Add in the all-purpose flour and ½ cup of the chicken broth into the bowl. Whisk until smooth in consistency.

4. In the same saucepan set over medium to high heat, add in the butter. Once melted, add in the chopped onions and sliced mushrooms. Cook for 5 minutes or until soft.

5. Add in the remaining chicken broth and flour mix. Allow to come to a boil. Cook for 3 minutes or until thick in consistency. Add in the whole milk. Season with a dash of black pepper. Add in the cooked rice and cooked sausage. Stir gently to mix. Cook for an additional minute.

6. Remove from heat and serve immediately.

Instructions:

1. In a stockpot set over medium to high heat, add in the olive oil. Add in the Italian turkey sausage links, chopped onion, chopped celery and chopped carrot. Cook for 8 to 10 minutes or until the turkey sausage is browned.

2. Add in the minced garlic. Cook for an additional minute.

3. Add in the chopped Swiss chard, chopped tomatoes, lay leaf, sage, Italian seasoning and black pepper. Stir gently to mix.

4. Add in the low sodium chicken broth. Allow to come to a boil. Lower the heat to low and cook for 10 to 12 minutes or until the chard is soft.

5. Add in the can of cannellini beans and lemon juice. Stir well until mixed.

6. Remove the bay leaf and remove from heat.

7. Serve immediately.

Recipe 14: Caribbean Sausage Chicken Stew

This is the perfect stew dish to make on the cold winter nights. It is so delicious, it will warm every inch of your body.

Yield: 8 servings

Preparation Time: 16 hours and 40 minutes

Ingredient List:

- ¼ cup of ketchup
- 3 cloves of garlic, minced
- 1 tablespoon of white sugar
- 1 tablespoon of hot sauce
- 1 teaspoon of browning sauce
- 1 teaspoon of dried basil
- 1 teaspoon of dried thyme
- 1 teaspoon of smoked paprika
- Dash of salt and black pepper
- ½ teaspoons of dried oregano
- ½ teaspoons of powdered allspice
- 8 chicken thighs, bone-in and skin removed
- 1 pound of andouille chicken sausage links, cooked and thinly sliced
- 1 onion, chopped
- 2 carrots, chopped
- 2 ribs of celery, chopped

HHHHHHHHHHHHHHHHHHHHHHHHHHHHHHH

Instructions:

1. In a Ziploc bag, add in the ketchup, minced garlic, white sugar, hot sauce, browning sauce, dried basil, dried thyme, smoked paprika, powdered allspice, dash of salt and dash of black pepper. Stir well to mix.

2. Add in the chicken thighs, chicken sausage links, chopped onion, chopped carrots and chopped celery into the Ziploc bag. Seal the bag and toss well to mix.

3. Place into the fridge to marinate for 8 hours.

4. Pour the mix into a slow cooker. Cover and cook on the lowest setting for 6 to 8 hours or until the chicken is soft.

5. Serve.

Recipe 15: Turkey and Sausage Cabbage Rolls

This is a dish I grew up with in my grandmother's kitchen and once you get a taste of it, it will have you thinking about your grandparents' cooking.

Yield: 12 servings

Preparation Time: 7 hours and 50 minutes

Ingredient List:

- 12 + 6 cabbage leaves
- 2, 3 ounce packs of instant multigrain rice mix
- 1 onion chopped
- ½ of a sweet red pepper, chopped
- ¼ cup of parsley, minced
- 3 teaspoons of Italian seasoning
- 1 ¼ teaspoons of salt
- 1 teaspoon of powdered garlic
- 1 teaspoon of black pepper
- 1 ½ pounds of lean ground turkey
- 3 Italian turkey sausage links, casings removed
- 1, 46-ounce bottle of V8 juice

HHHHHHHHHHHHHHHHHHHHHHHHHHHHHH

Instructions:

1. In a pot set over medium to high heat, fill with water. Allow to come to a boil. Add in the cabbage leaves. Cook for 5 minutes or until crispy. Drain and set aside to cool slightly.

2. In a bowl, add in the multigrain rice mix, chopped onion, chopped sweet red pepper, minced parsley, Italian seasoning, dash of salt, powdered garlic and black pepper. Stir well to mix.

3. In a slow cooker, add in the cabbage leaves to line the bottom. Top off with ½ cup of the filling mix. Cover with extra cabbage leaves and tuck the sides in to form rolls.

4. Pour the V8 juice over the top.

5. Cover and cook on the lowest setting for 7 to 9 hours or until the cabbage is soft.

6. Serve.

Recipe 16: Sausage and Mushroom Rigatoni

This is a rich and decadent sausage dish you can make whenever you need something especially filling. Serve with garlic bread for the tastiest results.

Yield: 6 servings

Preparation Time: 25 minutes

Ingredient List:

- 12 ounces of rigatoni pasta
- 12 ounces of Italian sausage
- 1 tablespoon of butter
- 1 pound of mushrooms, thinly sliced
- 2 cloves of garlic, minced
- ½ teaspoons of salt
- Dash of black pepper
- 2 cups of heavy whipping cream
- Parsley, minced and for topping

HHHHHHHHHHHHHHHHHHHHHHHHHHHHHHH

Instructions:

1. Prepare the rigatoni pasta according to the directions on the package. Drain the pasta and set aside.

2. In a skillet set over medium heat, add in the sausage. Cook for 4 to 6 minutes or until browned. Crumble the sausage and transfer onto a plate. Drain the excess grease.

3. In the same skillet, add in the butter. Once melted, add in the sliced mushrooms and minced garlic. Season with a dash of salt and black pepper. Cook for 5 minutes or until soft. Continue to cook for an additional 2 to 3 minutes.

4. Add in the heavy whipping cream. Allow to come to a boil. Lower the heat to low. Cook for 8 to 10 minutes or until thick in consistency.

5. Add the sausage back into the skillet along with the cooked pasta. Toss to coat.

6. Remove from heat.

7. Serve immediately with a garnish of minced parsley.

Recipe 17: Sausage Jambalaya

This is a tasty dish you don't have to feel guilty about enjoying. It is so delicious, you can easily make it any night of the week.

Yield: 4 servings

Preparation Time: 30 minutes

Ingredient List:

- 8 ounces of chicken breasts, boneless, skinless and cut into pieces
- 1 teaspoon of Cajun seasoning
- 2 teaspoons of extra virgin olive oil
- 6 ounces of smoked turkey sausage, thinly sliced
- 1 sweet red pepper, chopped
- 2 ribs of celery, chopped
- 1 onion, chopped
- ½ cup of no salt tomato sauce
- 1 cup of bulgur
- 1 cup of low sodium chicken broth
- ¾ cup of water
- ¼ teaspoons of cayenne pepper

HHHHHHHHHHHHHHHHHHHHHHHHHHHHHHH

Instructions:

1. In a bowl, add in the chicken breast pieces and Cajun seasoning. Toss well until coated.

2. In a saucepan set over medium heat, add in the olive oil. Add in the seasoned chicken. Cook for 2 to 3 minutes. Transfer the chicken onto a plate and set aside.

3. In the same saucepan, add in the smoked turkey sausage slices. Cook for 1 to 2 minutes or until browned. Add in the chopped sweet red pepper, chopped celery and chopped onion. Cook for 2 minutes.

4. Add in the no salt tomato sauce. Continue to cook for an additional 30 seconds.

5. Add in the bulgur, low sodium chicken broth, water and cooked chicken. Stir well to mix. Season with the cayenne pepper. Allow to come to a boil. Lower the heat to low. Cook for 10 minutes or until the bulgur is soft.

6. Remove from heat and serve immediately.

Recipe 18: Sausage and Egg Grits

This is a delicious early morning dish you can serve to pair along with your main breakfast meal. It is packed with a downhome flavor I know you will love.

Yield: 6 servings

Preparation Time: 35 minutes

Ingredient List:

- 4 turkey sausage links, casings removed
- 1 ½ cup of egg substitute
- 1 ¼ cups of whole milk, evenly divided
- 3 cups of water
- Dash of salt and black pepper
- 1 cup of quick cooking grits
- ¾ cup of low-fat cheddar cheese, shredded and evenly divided
- 2 green onions, chopped

HHHHHHHHHHHHHHHHHHHHHHHHHHHHHHHH

Instructions:

1. In a skillet set over medium heat, add in the sausage. Cook for 8 to 10 minutes or until browned. Transfer onto a plate lined with paper towels to drain. Drain the excess grease.

2. In a bowl, add in the egg substitute and ¼ cup of milk. Whisk until mixed. Pour into the skillet. Cook for 3 to 5 minutes or until the eggs are set. Remove from heat and set aside.

3. In a Dutch oven set over medium heat, add in the water, dash of salt ad whole milk. Allow to come to a boil. Add in the grits and stir well to incorporate. Lower the heat to low. Cook for 6 to 8 minutes or until thick in consistency.

4. Add in half of the shredded cheddar cheese. Add in the cooked sausage, cooked eggs and chopped green onions. Season with a dash of black pepper.

5. Remove from heat and serve immediately.

Recipe 19: Sausage and Egg Burritos

Whenever you are craving something on the healthy side, then this is one of the best dishes that you need to try for yourself.

Yield: 6 servings

Preparation Time: 20 minutes

Ingredient List:

- ½ pound of lean turkey sweet Italian sausage
- 3 eggs
- 4 egg whites
- 1 tablespoon of extra virgin olive oil
- 2 cups of spinach, chopped
- 2 plum tomatoes, seeds and chopped
- 1 clove of garlic, minced
- ¼ teaspoons of black pepper
- 6 whole wheat tortillas, warm
- Mild salsa, for topping

HHHHHHHHHHHHHHHHHHHHHHHHHHHHHHH

Instructions:

1. In a skillet, add in the Italian sausage. Cook for 5 to 7 minutes or until browned. Transfer onto a plate and set aside.

2. In a bowl, add in the eggs and egg whites. Whisk until lightly beaten. Add into the skillet. Cook for 3 to 5 minutes or until the eggs are cooked through. Transfer onto a plate. Wipe the skillet clean.

3. In the skillet, add in the olive oil. Add in the chopped spinach, chopped plum tomatoes and minced garlic. Cook for 2 to 3 minutes or until the spinach wilts. Add in the cooked sausage and eggs. Stir well to mix.

4. Season with a dash of black pepper.

5. Spoon 2/3 of the sausage mix onto each whole wheat tortilla.

6. Top off with the mild salsa.

7. Roll the tortillas into tight burritos. Serve immediately.

Recipe 20: Smoked Sausage and Potato Soup

This is a filling and savory soup dish you can make for those adults in your home. While it is made with only a small amount of beer, I guarantee every adult will love it.

Yield: 4 servings

Preparation Time: 30 minutes

Ingredient List:

- 1 pound of smoked sausage
- 2 Tablespoons of butter
- 1 onion, chopped
- 2 stalks of celery, chopped
- 3 cups of low sodium chicken broth
- 6 Russet potatoes, peeled and cut into small cubes
- 1 ½ pounds of Velveeta cheese, cut into cubes
- 1 cup of whole milk
- 1 cup of heavy whipping cream
- ½ cup of beer
- ¼ teaspoons of black pepper
- Parsley, chopped and for serving

HHHHHHHHHHHHHHHHHHHHHHHHHHHHHH

Instructions:

1. In a pot set over medium to high heat, add in the butter, chopped onion, chopped celery and smoked sausage. Stir well to mix. Cook for 5 minutes.

2. Add in the low sodium chicken broth and potato cubes. Allow to come to a boil. Lower the heat to low. Cook for 10 to 12 minutes.

3. Mash the potatoes with a potato masher.

4. Add in the whole milk, heavy whipping cream, beef, Velveeta cheese cubes and dash of black pepper. Stir well to incorporate. Continue to cook for an additional 10 minutes or until the cheese is melted.

5. Remove from heat.

6. Serve the soup with a garnish of chopped parsley.

Recipe 21: Italian Sausage and Potato Chowder

Make this delicious chowder whenever you are feeling under the weather. It is incredibly easy to make and is so delicious, I know you will want to make it as often as possible.

Yield: 4 servings

Preparation Time: 40 minutes

Ingredient List:

- ½ cup of yellow onion, chopped
- 1 pound of mild Italian sausage
- ½ teaspoons of extra virgin olive oil
- 4 cups of potato, peeled and chopped
- 3 cups of low sodium chicken stock
- 1 cup of celery, chopped
- 1 cup of heavy whipping cream
- 1 cup of sharp cheddar cheese, shredded

HHHHHHHHHHHHHHHHHHHHHHHHHHHHHH

Instructions:

1. In a saucepan set over medium heat, add in the olive oil. Add in the chopped onions. Cook for 5 minutes or until translucent.

2. Add in the Italian sausage. Cook for 8 to 10 minutes or until browned.

3. In a pot set over medium to high heat, add in the chopped potatoes, low sodium chicken stock and chopped celery. Allow to come to a boil. Lower the heat to medium. Cook for 20 minutes or until the potatoes are soft.

4. Transfer the sausage and onions into the soup pot.

5. Add in the heavy whipping cream and shredded cheddar cheese. Stir well to incorporate. Cook for 1 to 2 minutes.

6. Remove from heat and serve immediately.

Recipe 22: Apple and Sausage Salad with Vinaigrette

If you are craving something on the lighter side, then look no further. This is such an easy salad dish you can make, you can have it ready in just a matter of minutes.

Yield: 6 servings

Preparation Time: 35 minutes

Ingredient List:

- 4 slices of cinnamon and raisin bread
- 1/3 cup of extra virgin olive oil
- 3 Tablespoons of apple cider vinegar
- 2 teaspoons of honey
- ½ teaspoons of powdered cinnamon
- Dash of sea salt
- Dash of black pepper
- 1, 12-ounce pack of apple chicken sausage links, thinly sliced
- 2, 5-ounce packs of spring mix salad greens
- 2 cups of Bartlett pears, thinly sliced
- ½ cup of walnuts, toasted and chopped
- ½ cup of sweet cherries, dried

HHHHHHHHHHHHHHHHHHHHHHHHHHHHHH

Instructions:

1. Preheat the oven to 375 degrees.

2. Slice the bread slices into 12 cubes. Place into a baking dish. Place into the oven to bake for 8 to 10 minutes or until toasted. Remove and set aside to cool for 5 minutes.

3. In a bowl, add in the olive oil, apple cider vinegar, honey and powdered cinnamon. Season with a dash of sea salt and black pepper. Stir well until mixed.

4. In a skillet set over medium heat, add in the sliced apple chicken sausage. Cook for 2 to 3 minutes on each side or until browned.

5. Divide the salad greens onto 6 plates. Top off with the cooked sausage, Bartlett pear slices, chopped walnuts, dried sweet cherries and baked bread cubes.

6. Drizzle the dressing over the top.

7. Serve.

Recipe 23: Andouille Sausage Soup

This is the perfect soup dish to make for your next Sunday game night. It is packed full of plenty of veggies and sausage to make a filling dish everybody will love.

Yield: 10 servings

Preparation Time: 55 minutes

Ingredient List:

- 1 tablespoon of canola oil
- 2 onions, chopped
- 3 carrots, chopped
- 1 green bell pepper, seeds removed and chopped
- 2 cloves of garlic, minced
- 1, 12-ounce pack of andouille chicken sausage links, thinly sliced
- 1 ½ pounds of red potatoes, cut into cubes
- 1, 28 ounce can of tomatoes, crushed
- 1 teaspoon of Worcestershire sauce
- ¼ teaspoons of black pepper
- 1, 32-ounce carton of low sodium beef broth
- 2 teaspoons of liquid smoked
- ¼ teaspoons of cayenne pepper
- Sour cream, for serving

HHHHHHHHHHHHHHHHHHHHHHHHHHHHHHH

Instructions:

1. In a stockpot set over medium to high heat, add in the canola oil. Add in the chopped onions, chopped carrots and chopped green bell pepper. Stir well to mix. Cook for 8 to 10 minutes or until soft.

2. Add in the minced garlic. Cook for an additional minute. Transfer onto a plate and set aside.

3. In the same pot, add in the sliced andouille sausage. Cook for 8 minutes or until browned.

4. Add in the red potato cubes, Worcestershire sauce, crushed tomatoes, low sodium beef broth and onion mix. Season with a dash of black pepper.

5. Add in the liquid smoked and cayenne pepper. Allow to come to a boil. Lower the heat to low and cover. Cook for 15 to 20 minutes or until soft.

6. Remove from heat. Serve with a topping of sour cream.

Recipe 24: One Pot Cajun Chicken and Sausage Alfredo

This is the perfect sausage dish for you to make whenever you want to impress your friends and family with your cooking skills.

Yield: 8 to 10 servings

Preparation Time: 35 minutes

Ingredient List:

- 4 Tablespoons of extra virgin olive oil
- 1 pound of chicken, cut into pieces
- ½ teaspoons of salt
- Dash of black pepper
- 14 ounces of smoked sausage, thinly sliced
- 4 cloves of garlic, minced
- 1 quart of low sodium chicken broth
- 2 ½ cups of heavy whipping cream
- 1 pound of penne pasta
- 1 ½ Tablespoons of Cajun seasoning, extra for topping
- 4 ounces of parmesan cheese, shredded
- 1 cup of flat leaf parsley, minced

HHHHHHHHHHHHHHHHHHHHHHHHHHHHHHH

Instructions:

1. Season the chicken pieces with a dash of salt and black pepper.

2. In a pot set over medium to high heat, add in the olive oil. Add in the seasoned chicken pieces. Cook for 8 to 10 minutes or until browned.

3. Add in the sliced sausage. Continue to cook for 5 minutes or until browned.

4. Add in the minced garlic and cook for an additional minute.

5. Add in the low sodium chicken broth, heavy whipping cream, penne pasta and Cajun seasoning. Stir well to mix. Allow to come to a simmer. Lower the heat to low. Cover and cook for 15 to 20 minutes or until the pasta is soft.

6. Remove from heat.

7. Add in the shredded parmesan cheese and minced parsley. Stir well to incorporate.

8. Serve immediately.

Recipe 25: One Pan Smoked Sausage and Pasta

This is a delicious sausage dish you can make whenever you need something both easy and mess-free to make. Since it is made in one pot, it really doesn't get any easier than this.

Yield: 4 servings

Preparation Time: 25 minutes

Ingredient List:

- 1 tablespoon of extra virgin olive oil
- 1 pound of sausage, thinly sliced
- ½ cup of onion, chopped
- 1 tablespoon of garlic, minced
- 2 cups of low sodium chicken broth
- 1, 14 ounce can of tomatoes, chopped
- ½ cup of whole milk
- 8 ounces of bow tie pasta
- Dash of salt and black pepper
- 2 cups of cheddar cheese, shredded
- ¼ teaspoons of crushed red pepper flakes
- 1/3 cup of scallions, chopped

HHHHHHHHHHHHHHHHHHHHHHHHHHHHHH

Instructions:

1. In a pot set over medium to high heat, add in the olive oil. Add in the chopped onion and sliced Italian sausage. Stir well to mix. Cook for 5 minutes.

2. Add in the minced garlic, dash of black pepper and crushed red pepper flakes. Stir well to mix. Cook for an additional minute.

3. Add in the low sodium chicken broth, chopped tomatoes, whole milk and bow tie pasta. Stir well to mix. Allow to come to a boil. Lower the heat to medium. Cook for 15 minutes or until the pasta is soft.

4. Add in the shredded cheddar cheese. Stir well to mix. Cook for 1 to 2 minutes or until melted.

5. Remove from heat.

6. Serve immediately with a garnish of chopped scallions.

About the Author

Angel Burns learned to cook when she worked in the local seafood restaurant near her home in Hyannis Port in Massachusetts as a teenager. The head chef took Angel under his wing and taught the young woman the tricks of the trade for cooking seafood. The skills she had learned at a young age helped her get accepted into Boston University's Culinary Program where she also minored in business administration.

Summers off from school meant working at the same restaurant but when Angel's mentor and friend retired as head chef, she took over after graduation and created classic and new dishes that delighted the diners. The restaurant flourished under Angel's culinary creativity and one customer developed more than an appreciation for Angel's food. Several months after taking over the position, the young woman met her future husband at work and they have been inseparable ever since. They still live in Hyannis Port with their two children and a cocker spaniel named Buddy.

Angel Burns turned her passion for cooking and her business acumen into a thriving e-book business. She has authored several successful books on cooking different types of dishes using simple ingredients for novices and experienced chefs alike. She is still head chef in Hyannis Port and says she will probably never leave!

Author's Afterthoughts

With so many books out there to choose from, I want to thank you for choosing this one and taking precious time out of your life to buy and read my work. Readers like you are the reason I take such passion in creating these books.

It is with gratitude and humility that I express how honored I am to become a part of your life and I hope that you take the same pleasure in reading this book as I did in writing it.

Can I ask one small favour? I ask that you write an honest and open review on Amazon of what you thought of the book. This will help other readers make an informed choice on whether to buy this book.

My sincerest thanks,

Angel Burns

If you want to be the first to know about news, new books, events and giveaways, subscribe to my newsletter by clicking the link below

https://angel-burns.gr8.com

or Scan QR-code